CAPTURED
HISTORY

BREAKER BOYS

HOW A PHOTOGRAPH HELPED END CHILD LABOR

by Michael Burgan

Content Adviser: Brett Barker, PhD,
Associate Professor of History,
University of Wisconsin–Marathon County

COMPASS POINT BOOKS
a capstone imprint

Compass Point Books
151 Good Counsel Drive
P.O. Box 669
Mankato, MN 56002-0669

Managing Editor: Catherine Neitge
Designer: Tracy Davies
Media Researcher: Wanda Winch
Library Consultant: Kathleen Baxter
Production Specialist: Sarah Bennett

Image Credits

Courtesy Janet Lindenmuth, 14; Getty Images Inc: George Eastman House, 25, 51;
Johnstown Area Heritage Association (JAHA), 17; Lewis Hine. *A Cotton Warper,
Shelton Looms, ca. 1933. Industrial Life Photograph Collection. Baker Library
Historical Collections. Harvard Business School (olvwork390899), 50; Library of
Congress: Prints and Photographs Division, cover, 5, 6, 7, 8, 11, 19, 20, 22, 27, 29,
30, 31, 32, 33, 34, 35, 37, 38, 41, 42, 43, 44, 45, 46, 47, 49, 54, 56 (bottom), 57
(all), 58 (all), 59; New York Public Library: Astor, Lenox and Tilden Foundations/
Miriam and Ira D. Wallach Division of Art, Prints and Photographs, Photography
Collection/Lewis W. Hine, 53; Timothy Hughes Rare & Early Newspapers, 13, 56 (top)

Library of Congress Cataloging-in-Publication Data

Burgan, Michael.
  Breaker boys: how a photograph helped end child labor / written by Michael Burgan.
    p. cm.—(Captured history)
  Includes bibliographical references and index.
  ISBN 978-0-7565-4439-3 (library binding)
  ISBN 978-0-7565-4510-9 (paperback)
  1. Hine, Lewis Wickes, 1874–1940—Juvenile literature. 2. Child labor—United
States—History—Juvenile literature. 3. Coal mines and mining—Pennsylvania—
History—Juvenile literature. 4. Child labor—United States—History—Pictorial
works—Juvenile literature. 5. Documentary photography—United States—History—
Juvenile literature. I. Title.
HD6250.U3B87 2012
331.3'10973—dc22   2011003316

Visit Compass Point Books on the Internet at *www.capstonepub.com*

Printed in the United States of America in North Mankato, Minnesota.
082011   006326R

TABLEOFCONTENTS

ChapterOne
COAL WAS KING

The breakers sat on hills across northeastern Pennsylvania, towering over other buildings nearby. To some people, their sloping shapes made them look a little like ancient monuments—part of a pyramid, perhaps. To writer Stephen Crane, the huge structures presented a darker picture. He said they "squatted upon the hillsides and in the valley like enormous preying monsters, eating of the sunshine, the grass, the green leaves."

The breakers were the most noticeable buildings at the collieries of northeastern Pennsylvania. There miners dug anthracite coal from the earth and prepared it for shipping to market. Inside the breakers coal was broken into small pieces and separated from other rocks that had been dug up with it.

For a time during the 1800s and early 1900s, coal was king in many parts of Pennsylvania. Mine owners made huge fortunes providing the hard, black fuel. And the mines created jobs for countless men throughout the region and other parts of the United States. The work, though, was difficult—and dangerous. And men weren't the only ones who risked their health or their lives bringing the coal to waiting customers. Some boys, especially older ones, worked in the mines. Many more boys worked in the breakers, sorting jagged chunks of coal by hand and breathing the black dust the machinery

"They squatted upon the hillsides and in the valley like enormous preying monsters."

A Pennsylvania coal breaker loomed over the workers.

spewed into the air. These youngsters, called breaker boys, were usually the sons of miners who worked deep underground. The boys were mostly unknown outside their small hometowns. But the camera of Lewis Hine helped change that.

Hine, an investigative photographer, arrived at the coal mines around South Pittston, Pennsylvania, in January 1911. He had already spent several years traveling across

Breaker boy Angelo Ross told photographer Lewis Hine in 1911 that he was 13. Hine didn't believe he was that old.

America, photographing the nation's children at work. Child labor was an important issue to some Americans. Factory owners hired children because they could pay them less than adults. The children took the jobs so they could help support their families and gain experience. Boys in coal country grew up knowing they would most likely work in the mines, like their fathers.

But from about 1890 to 1920 a group of Americans known as Progressives tried to stop the use of children in the work force—especially in dangerous industries, such as coal mining. Children, the Progressives believed, should be educated and protected—not given difficult and sometimes deadly jobs.

PROGRESSIVES UNITED TO HELP CHILDREN

Sadie Pfeifer was one of many small children photographed by Lewis Hine working in a South Carolina cotton mill.

During the 1800s America and the world turned more and more to machines to make goods and provide transportation. This was the age of the Industrial Revolution. Immigrants flocked to the United States to work in factories, mills, and mines. While the rise of industries created great wealth for some Americans, others faced harsh working and living conditions.

Around 1890 people who wanted to end suffering and help the poor became active in U.S. society. They did not always share the same goals or methods, but together they were known as Progressives. Some tried to help immigrants find jobs and learn English. Others tried to give all Americans a greater role in politics. Many tried to regulate how businesses were run, so they could not harm their workers or the public. During the Progressive era, which lasted until around 1920, the federal government became more involved in many areas of public life—including the use of children as workers.

Lewis Hine's photos of Pennsylvania breaker boys helped change labor law in the U.S.

Hine was a committed Progressive. He wanted all Americans to understand the dangers of child labor, and to see that it forced children to act like adults at too early an age. Hine once said he wanted "to make ... the whole country so sick and tired of the whole business" of child labor that it would become a thing of the past.

In and around South Pittston, Hine visited breaker boys in their neighborhoods. On January 10 he went to the Ewen Breaker, which was owned by the Pennsylvania Coal Company. Hine photographed the boys inside the breaker, hunched over the coal. He took pictures of them when they stopped for lunch. And he gathered a group of them outside the Ewen Breaker and took a picture that millions of Americans would eventually see. The photo showed boys of many ages and sizes, dressed in almost the same way. The breaker boys in Hine's photo were children sent to do a dirty, dangerous job. This photo, and others Hine took in the breakers and elsewhere across the country, helped spark a change. More people began to agree with the Progressives—child labor was wrong and had to end.

Chapter Two

COAL AND KIDS

Simple black rocks, formed millions of years ago, have provided people with fuel for centuries. Coal is plentiful in many parts of the United States, sometimes close to the surface, sometimes a few thousand feet below it. Before Europeans reached North America, the Pueblo Indians found coal and burned it to cook food and make pottery. In 1673 French explorers found coal along the Mississippi River, and several decades later, it was discovered near the James River in Virginia. That region became the site of the first commercial coal operation in what would become the United States.

The demand for coal led Americans to look for more sources, and they easily found them as they moved westward. The biggest need for coal came when the United States and much of the rest of the world began to industrialize. Coal created the heat that fueled steam engines, which in turn powered machines of all kinds. Steam power, based on coal, propelled the first trains. Later, after the Civil War, a material made from coal called coke became essential for making steel. During the 1870s and 1880s, U.S. coal production quadrupled as the demand continued to rise. Soon coal would also become a source of power for the plants that generated electricity.

When the first settlers came to the area around South Pittston, Pennsylvania, they found a region rich with coal.

During the 1870s and 1880s, U.S. coal production quadrupled as the demand continued to rise.

Hine photographed boys and men at work deep in the Pittston mine.

The type of coal there is called anthracite. The first miners soon discovered that anthracite was hard to light. But once lit, it burned longer and more cleanly than other coal, and it provided a strong heat. Mining anthracite became a major industry in northeastern Pennsylvania, where a region covering about 500 square miles (1,295 square kilometers) contained almost three-quarters of the world's known supply of anthracite.

Although some anthracite coal was found near the earth's surface, most of it was much deeper. Mining companies dug long shafts into the sides of hills or straight down into the ground. Large timbers lined the roofs and walls of the shafts to hold up the dirt and rocks. Deep underground, water often flowed into the shafts. Pumps kept most of the water out, but the miners still sometimes worked in knee-deep water.

The job presented many dangers. Miners used explosives to break off the coal from the surrounding rock. If miners mishandled the explosives, they could easily die in an accidental blast. The timbers holding back the earth and rock could break, causing a collapse that could kill the miners or cut off their route back to the surface. Or parts of the mine could fill with methane, a gas released by coal. In the days before batteries, miners carried lamps with open flames to see their way in the dark mines. A spark from a lamp could cause the methane to explode, killing everyone nearby. Other gases found in the mines could kill even without a spark because breathing them was deadly.

No government agencies then protected workers doing dangerous jobs. Many Americans believed that government should not interfere with how companies ran their businesses. And the companies used their political influence in some states to prevent the creation of safety laws. Finally the growing number of disasters and deaths led the U.S. government to force companies to improve mine safety.

Even if the miners survived working in the mines, many faced a long-term health risk. Over time the dust

Gases found in the mines could kill even without a spark because breathing them was deadly.

THE AVONDALE FIRE

A sketch on the cover of the September 25, 1869, issue of Harper's Weekly *was captioned "The Avondale Colliery disaster—bringing out the dead."*

The deadliest mining disaster in the anthracite region occurred in September 1869 near Scranton, Pennsylvania. In the Avondale mine, sparks from a furnace torched wooden beams in a shaft, and the fire quickly burned out of control. The death toll of 110 included two rescuers and five boys who worked at the mine. *The New York Times* described the scene: "... in a short time the whole breaker and outbuildings were in flames, and the hoisting apparatus, the only means of escape for the miners, destroyed. All efforts to stay [stop] the flames were in vain, and the whole structure fell, partly filling the shaft. ... The work of quenching the fire and clearing the shaft consumed some hours, and in the meanwhile thousands of people gathered from the surrounding country. The families of the men in the pit were soon present, and their cries were heart-rending in the extreme."

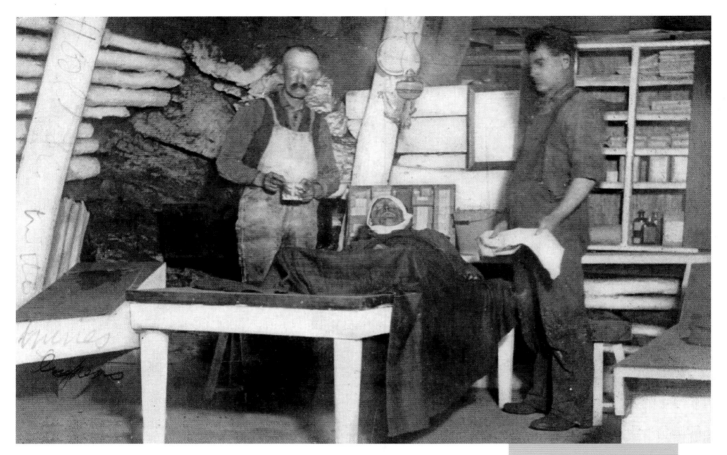

An injured man was treated in an emergency hospital inside a Pennsylvania mine in 1906.

from the coal collected in their lungs, causing black lung disease. The disease makes it hard to breathe and can lead to other lung diseases that can kill, such as emphysema. About three-fourths of miners eventually developed black lung disease—if they didn't die in the mines first. By one estimate, three miners died every two days in the anthracite mines of Pennsylvania. Improvements in technology and laws to protect workers slowly lowered the numbers. But even in the middle of the 20th century, on average one miner a day was killed in a U.S. coal mine.

Starting in the 1820s, immigrants came to the

anthracite region of Pennsylvania to work in the mines. At first most came from the United Kingdom and what is now Germany. Many had worked in European coal mines. In the late 1830s, Irish immigrants began coming to the area in large numbers. From the mid-1840s to the mid-1850s, more than 1.5 million left their homeland to escape a severe famine. Many found work doing difficult jobs that native-born Americans avoided. Starting in the late 1880s, more immigrants came from southern and eastern Europe. Soon men from what are now the Czech Republic and Slovakia found work in the mines of northeastern Pennsylvania. So did Italians, Poles, and immigrants from many other nations.

It was hard for many of the immigrants to adjust to life in a new land. They didn't speak English, and most were uneducated. Many were not Protestants, which was the dominant faith in the United States at the time. The languages, customs, and religions of the Catholic and Jewish newcomers struck many Americans as odd—or threatening. Many immigrants faced prejudice as they looked for places to live. Some lived in barns, while others lived in small rooms with as many as five other people.

But one thing the immigrants could usually find in Pennsylvania's coal country was a job at a colliery. For a man with no skills, coal mining paid better than most other work. The newcomers overlooked the dangers, hoping to save enough money to buy their own home, or perhaps a farm. And the mine owners prized the attitudes that the best of the workers brought with them. One

Many immigrants faced prejudice as they looked for places to live.

writer described the typical Slavic miner around 1900: "He is obedient and amenable to discipline, courageous and willing to work, [having much] physical strength and capable of great physical endurance."

No matter where they came from, most miners settled in small villages known as patch towns. The villages were owned by the mining companies. The companies rented housing to the workers and owned the stores where miners and their families shopped. The companies followed a practice called "mining the miners"—they tried to collect back as much of the pay they gave the miners as they could. The companies charged high rents, and prices in the company stores were often steep compared with prices in other towns' stores. The miners shopped at the company stores anyway, because stores with lower prices were often too far away. And the company store would let miners buy on credit, which other stores often refused to do. Sometimes the miners had no choice—they were paid in "scrip," not cash. Scrip could only be spent at the company store.

So at work miners faced the constant threat of injury or death. At home they faced difficult conditions in the poorly made, overpriced houses that filled the patch towns. Still the immigrants thought life was better in Pennsylvania than it had been in Europe. In their homelands many of the immigrants had lacked political rights, and they were forced to serve in the military. In America they had more freedom and free education for their children. And most

Miners' families crowded into rundown housing without indoor plumbing.

believed they could create a better life for their families in America.

The dream of improving their lives and their children's lives—the American Dream—drove many immigrants to the United States. But across the country, not just in the anthracite coal region, children often had to work to help their families survive. Child labor was not new. For thousands of years, children had worked next to their parents on family farms. They had learned the skills needed to run a household or to make goods or provide services to sell to others. But the Industrial Revolution brought a new kind of child labor. Working children often spent the day away from their parents, and their bosses in a factory or mill had little concern about their health or safety.

As early as the 1780s, children worked in mills that produced textiles. Some were as young as 5 years old. In 1817 a popular news magazine noted that factory work was "better done by little girls from six to twelve years old" than by grown men. Factory owners could pay children less than adults, and children were less likely to challenge the owners over long workdays or harsh working conditions.

In some states lawmakers worried about the spread of child labor. Not because the children were treated badly, though they often were, but because working kept the children out of school. In 1813 Connecticut became the first of several states to require that working children also be given schooling at the workplace. Other laws required that working children under 15 receive at least three months of education a year.

During the 1800s boys as young as 6 took their first job in the breakers, sorting through the coal. Many worked 10 hours a day, six days per week. For their 10 hours of work, the breaker boys earned as little as 45 cents—less than half of what adults were paid. In the earliest days, before machinery helped do some of the work, the rooms where the boys sorted coal filled with thick dust. The boys could barely see more than a few feet. And the dust, over time, often led to black lung disease. The mechanical breakers were somewhat

During the 19th century, boys as young as 6 took their first job in the breakers, sorting through the coal.

Many of the breaker boys Hine photographed suffered from chronic coughs.

cleaner. But the machinery shook the whole building and filled the breaker with constant loud noise.

The efforts to place some limits on child labor continued through the 1800s. But the movement picked up steam with the appearance of the Progressives. Reformers wanted to help immigrants adjust to life in America and end poverty. One solution, some Progressives thought, was making sure immigrant children were educated. That meant taking them out of factories and mines and putting them in schools. The Progressives

INSIDE THE "MONSTER"

Huge coal breaker in Westmoreland County, Pennsylvania, in 1905

In 1894 Stephen Crane had just completed his novel *The Red Badge of Courage*. The book explored the horrors of war through the eyes of a young Civil War private named Henry. While trying to get the book published, Crane visited a Pennsylvania coal mine and wrote about it for *McClure's Magazine.* He was angry about the heavily edited version of his article that was printed. He believed the magazine had left out much of his reporting to make the mines seem safer than they were. Here is an excerpt from his article that did make it into the magazine. It describes the work that went on inside a breaker:

"At the top of the 'breaker,' laborers were dumping the coal into chutes. The huge lumps slid slowly on their journey down through the building, from which they were to emerge in classified fragments. Great teeth on revolving cylinders caught them and chewed them. At places there were grates that bid each size go into its proper chute. The dust lay inches deep on every motionless thing, and clouds of it made the air dark as from a violent tempest. A mighty gnashing sound filled the ears. With terrible appetite this huge and hideous monster sat ... munching coal, grinding its mammoth jaws with unearthly and monotonous uproar."

pressured state governments to act, and they hoped the federal government in Washington, D.C., would respond as well. The effort usually involved setting a minimum age for children to begin working in mines or factories, such as 14 or 16. The Progressives also wanted all children to attend school for at least eight years, with some also calling for four years of high school.

An event in 1902 focused national attention on child labor in the anthracite mines of northeastern Pennsylvania. Coal miners went on strike. They wanted better pay and safer working conditions. About 147,000 colliery workers stopped working, which meant no pay for them and their families. Some men, desperate for money, agreed to work for the mines, and they were attacked by the strikers.

As the Great Strike of 1902 went on, Americans saw how many of the workers were boys. Pennsylvania state law limited the age of mine workers. Boys had to be at least 12 to work in a breaker or at another job on the surface. They had to be a few years older to work underground in the mines. But Pennsylvania did not enforce the laws, and many parents submitted false evidence of their sons' ages. The parents needed the money the boys could make in the breakers or the mines. At the time of the strike, almost 20 percent of the anthracite workers were not legally old enough to be working at the mines.

Child labor became an important issue for more

Americans. The 1900 U.S. Census had shown that 1.75 million children from age 10 to 15 worked outside the home. That was 6 percent of all workers. In 1904 a group of Progressives formed the National Child Labor Committee (NCLC) to bring more attention to the problem and fight for reform. Its first target was the anthracite coal industry.

The next year NCLC president Owen Lovejoy visited the mines of northeastern Pennsylvania. He wrote reports about the boys he saw working there. The door boys, called

Hine wrote in 1911 that 13-year-old Willie had a lonely job as a nipper, waiting by the doors of the mine. False papers submitted to the mine said Willie was 16.

nippers, tended large wooden doors between sections of the mines. Others took care of the mules used to haul wagonloads of coal out of the mines. But most of the youngest workers were breaker boys. Lovejoy pointed out some of the dangers the boys faced—"in the coal breakers little boys are sometimes ground in the large crushers that break the coal, caught in the wheels or other machinery, or buried in a stream of coal." But Lovejoy also worried about how the work affected the boys' characters. They lacked proper schooling and spent time around men with such bad habits as swearing, gambling, and drinking alcohol. He feared that "the lives of many of the small boys in the coal region are already so tainted by vicious habits that an almost insuperable obstacle to a maturity of virtue and intelligence is presented."

Owen Lovejoy used words in the battle against child labor. Several years later another member of the NCLC chose a different weapon when he visited coal country— his camera.

ChapterThree
CHANGING THE WORLD

Even before joining the National Child Labor Committee, Lewis Hine knew something about child labor. As a teenager he had helped support his family by working in a furniture factory. Years later in New York, he taught science and geography to children. Hine, like other Progressives, saw education as the way to give children a better chance to live full, meaningful lives. Sending them off to mills and mines robbed them of this chance.

Hine bought his first camera in 1903 while teaching in New York. He quickly realized the potential for photography to reveal the truth and to teach—and to change the world. With a camera, he and others could show people what life was like for immigrants, the poor, and the children working in factories. Hine eventually called himself a social photographer. He sometimes became angry with photographers who took only pictures of wealthy people or pretty scenery. He wanted people to see his photos and take action to correct social problems.

Starting in 1907, when he was in his early 30s, Hine worked part time for the NCLC as a photographer. A year later he left teaching to work for the group full time. His job was to document the lives of child workers, both at home and in mines, factories, and mills. It was a difficult task in many ways. Cameras then were heavy, not like the small digital cameras of today. Hine had to lug up to

He wanted people to see his photos and take action to correct social problems.

Hine photographed
children in a slum
in 1910.

50 pounds (23 kilograms) of equipment with him to each
workplace. And the film he used was slow, meaning he
could not take clear pictures of anything that moved.
He had to ask his subjects to pose for him and remain
still while he took the picture.

Perhaps most difficult of all, Hine often had to pretend
to be someone he was not. Company owners usually did
not want the world outside to see the working conditions

in mines, factories and mills—especially the conditions for children. Hine sometimes told the bosses he simply wanted to photograph their equipment. Then he asked a child to stand in the picture, to show the size of the machinery compared with the young worker. Other times Hine said he was a fire inspector or a salesman. He learned how to take notes on a pad hidden in a coat pocket, so no one could see what he was doing. The notes included the ages and names of the children he photographed, and details about their working conditions. But the camera was his main tool. "If I could tell the story in words," he once said, "I wouldn't need to lug a camera."

A picture, he knew, could stir emotions in a way words could not.

Some of Hine's first photographs for the NCLC were of children working in glass factories and cotton mills. Then in 1911 he went to the anthracite region of Pennsylvania. Not much had changed since Owen Lovejoy's visit of 1905. Parents still turned in false records to show that their boys were old enough to work as breaker boys or miners. Hine learned that a few years before he arrived, a 10-year-old had fallen off a breaker, plunging to his death. The paperwork the boy had used to get the job said he was 14.

Hine also learned about the death of an older breaker boy. He wrote, "While I was in the region, two breaker boys of 15 ... fell or were carried by the coal down into the car below. One was badly burned and the other was smothered to death."

"If I could tell the story in words," he once said, "I wouldn't need to lug a camera."

BEFORE LEWIS HINE

An 1888 Jacob Riis photo captured three young boys sleeping in a New York City stairway.

Lewis Hine was not the only important photographer of the collieries or of the Progressive era. Before him, two other notable photographers showed the lives of immigrants and people working under difficult conditions. Starting in the 1870s, George Bretz took many photos of anthracite miners in Pennsylvania. His greatest fame came for pictures he took inside mines. Electric lights connected to a generator let Bretz capture images underground. Bretz also took some of the first photos of breaker boys at work. Unlike Hine, however, Bretz was not trying to right what he saw as a wrong. He was just taking photos.

Jacob Riis was more like Lewis Hine. Starting in the late 1880s, Riis took photographs of ordinary people in the poor neighborhoods of New York City. He showed many of the pictures at public lectures, and others were published in newspapers and magazines. Riis published some of the photos in 1890 in a book called *How the Other Half Lives,* a title that referred to the poor people many Americans never saw. Riis used his photos to try to persuade the wealthy to do more to help improve conditions for the poor.

A few days after that horrible accident, Hine reached the South Pittston area. On Sunday, January 8, he visited homes in the patch towns outside the local mines. He took pictures of several groups of breaker boys, dressed in their best clothes for church or a family gathering. He asked them their names and ages. He wrote in his notes that some of the boys were suspicious of him and why he was there. They feared he wanted to take them out of the colliery and put them in school. Sam Topent told Hine he had been working as a breaker boy for two years. "I'm 14 years," he said, "an' if you don' believe me, I kin show you de proofs." When other boys told him their ages, Hine couldn't believe what he heard. To the former teacher, most of them seemed younger than they claimed to be. Even if they were 12 or 13, they had obviously received little schooling. One boy who claimed to be 12 couldn't even spell his own name.

On January 10 Hine went to the Ewen Breaker in South Pittston. Sam Topent and the other boys he had photographed on Sunday worked there. Hine saw for himself the work the boys did and the conditions in the breaker. Coal moved from the top of the breaker down chutes. The boys sat over the chutes on planks of wood, one boy lower than the next. Whatever slate and other rocks the boys on the upper levels missed, the ones below them were supposed to catch. Slate looked similar to coal, so the boys had to bend over to closely inspect the moving rocks. They had gloves to protect their hands, but in some

They had gloves to protect their hands, but in some breakers the bosses wouldn't let boys wear them.

Breaker boys (from left) Philip Kurato, Jo Tabone, and Charlie Bootha posed for Lewis Hine in their best clothes in 1911. Charlie didn't know how to spell his name.

breakers the bosses wouldn't let boys wear them. The gloves made it harder to pick out smaller rocks. Even with the gloves, jagged edges sometimes pierced the cloth and cut the boys' hands.

Hine saw the thick coal dust that filled the breaker. He wrote that it went so deep into the boys' lungs "that for long periods after the boy leaves the breaker, he continues to cough up the black coal dust." Years before, a foreman at one of the anthracite mines had told Owen Lovejoy that with 20 boys in a breaker, "I bet you could shovel fifty

Hine photographed men and boys crowded into an elevator cage that took them to the surface.

pounds of dust out of their systems." The foreman was stretching the truth to make a point—the breaker boys were breathing a lot of coal dust.

For several hours, Hine later wrote, "I took a number of photos of the Breaker-boys at work ... and outside at the noon hour." The boys liked to play around the breaker at lunchtime, but that practice had recently stopped, Hine learned. A boy told him the bosses had ended the play after someone had hurt himself on the machinery. Besides, the boys weren't there to play; they were there to work.

Inside the breaker Hine photographed the boys on their

Hine's camera captured the breaker boys at work. He wrote that "the dust penetrates the utmost recesses of the boys' lungs."

planks, sorting through the coal. The photos show the dust swirling in the air. In the background light comes through several small windows, but the rest of the scene is dark. Hine photographed just what he saw and did not change his pictures afterward. He did not want to be accused of any fakery. Just a few months before his visit to the anthracite region, Hine wrote that his photos of child labor "have already set the authorities to see if 'such things can be possible.' They try to get around them by crying 'fake,' but therein lies the value of data and a witness." Hine, with his camera, was the witness, revealing the truth of child labor.

Hine carefully worked on his presentation. Inside the breaker he used just enough light to get his shot. He wanted the darkness to suggest the dark conditions in the breaker and the hard work that went on there. He also added captions to provide more information than a viewer could get from the photos alone. One photo of the boys at work shows a man standing near them. He holds a rod in his hand. "A kind of slave driver sometimes stands over the boys," Hine wrote, "prodding or kicking them into obedience."

At noon the boys stopped their work. While still sitting

Hine called the mine worker holding a rod (right) "a kind of slave driver."

on their planks, they turned toward Hine, and he took another picture. Then, for several shots, Hine had the boys stand in rows. The pictures he took with the boys like this provided the famous image that seemed to sum up the hard life of the breaker boys. Their faces are young, but they dress like grown workmen, with their jackets and overalls. Coal dust covers some of the faces, and the boys don't smile. They simply stare at the lens of Hine's camera. They show none of the joy most people associate with childhood—a joy the Progressives thought they deserved.

Hine's caption read: "Noon hour at the Ewen Breaker, Pennsylvania Coal Co."

But with the long workdays and harsh conditions in the breakers, the boys had nothing to be joyful about.

Many photographers then did not want their subjects to look at the camera. It made it too obvious to the viewer that the subjects knew a photographer was there and a picture was being made. But Hine often had his subjects look at him. He wanted the subject and the viewer to know that he was trying to capture reality.

Some of the boys Hine photographed at the Ewen Breaker were the same ones he had shot a few days before. But in his caption he does not name any of the boys in the picture. They are simply part of the many boys sent to breakers across the region. They represent all the breaker boys—and all the children everywhere who were sent to do adults' work.

Hine went to several breakers on his trip and photographed other boys. In one picture a group of boys is far away from the camera. At that distance they seem almost faceless. With Hine's famous image of the breaker boys, viewers can see individual faces and expressions.

Hine did not identify the breaker boys in his famous photo of the boys at work, but he did name the breaker boys he photographed away from the mines: Sam Bellom (from left), Sam Topent, James Ritz, Mikey Captan, and Tony Captan.

They can feel more of a connection to the boys—and to their lives. Across northeastern Pennsylvania and other coal-producing regions, many boys faced this difficult life. Modern scholars have written that this and other Hine photos make viewers feel sorry for the boys. Yet the harsh conditions also can make viewers want to look away or deny that such a reality exists. Hine hoped the range of emotions would lead people to take action—to do something to end child labor.

Hine had talked with bosses at the mines and other companies. He saw that their main concern was making money, not providing safe working conditions for children, let alone ending child labor. But showing his photos to average Americans might lead them to ask lawmakers to force the mine owners to at least obey the laws that already existed. At the same time, Hine knew photography was art, and using certain mixtures of light and dark and carefully composing the images would create the most impact on the viewer.

The breaker boys weren't the only youths Hine saw in anthracite country. He photographed the nippers and wrote about the boredom of their job. A nipper, Hine said, would sit alone for nine or 10 hours a day "in absolute darkness, save for his little oil lamp and the lamps of the passers-by; breathing air that is far from fresh air, fouled by smoking oil lamps and loaded with moisture." Hine also photographed boys who were drivers, and worked with mules. Even that work could be dangerous. Hine

A nipper, Hine said, would sit alone for nine or 10 hours a day "in absolute darkness, save for his little oil lamp and the lamps of the passers-by."

wrote that a boy "showed me where a mule had just kicked him when he wasn't looking."

After his short stay in South Pittston, Hine went across the country, taking more pictures of children at work. He photographed "newsies," the boys—and a few girls—who sold newspapers on city streets. He saw children working on farms and inside all sorts of factories. Hine continued working for the NCLC until 1918, traveling a total of 100,000 miles as he crisscrossed the country. He took more than 7,000 pictures of American children at work. Many of

THE INJURED AND THE DEAD

Neil Gallagher, 17, a former Pennsylvania breaker boy, lost his leg in a mining accident when he was 13. He was looking for work in New York when Hine photographed him in 1909.

While in Pennsylvania's coal country, Lewis Hine collected information about breaker boys and other children killed or badly injured while working. Some of the information appeared in a report he later wrote:

"1. Charles Nojenski

About 15 years of age. Caught in breakery machinery while throwing coal at other boys, and killed. The Company is [cleared] from all blame in the matter.

2. Joseph Martonik

About 15 years of age. Caught in the machinery and horribly mangled. Aug. 31, 1910 at Cranberry Colliery. If he had obeyed instructions, or if the machinery had been properly protected, the accident might not have happened.

3. Thomas Caffrey

Fourteen years old. A door-tender at #9 Colliery, Sugar Notch, Pa. Was assisting in hauling a trip and was jammed and killed, January 4th, 1910."

"The breaker boys ... came to symbolize all that was wrong with child labor."

the pictures appeared in magazines or were shown during lectures. Historian Walter Trattner wrote that the photos "aroused public sentiment against child labor in a way that no printed page or public lecture could."

But it was the pictures of the breaker boys that stayed in the minds of many Americans—the blackened faces and mostly blank stares of boys who spent their days breathing coal dust and trying to catch moving rocks with their hands. The boys who, with their parents' help, lied about their ages to make money for their families. Breaker boys such as Sam Topent, Tony Captan, and Charlie Bootha— whom Hine had met near their homes. They would go through life uneducated and with little hope of ever doing anything except working in the mines. As historian Hugh D. Hindman wrote, "The breaker boys, who endured some of the most grueling conditions among child workers anywhere, came to symbolize all that was wrong with child labor."

ChapterFour
ENDING CHILD LABOR

Lewis Hine's photos of the Pennsylvania breaker boys are famous today. But in the early 1900s, it was his total portfolio of child labor pictures that had the greatest effect. The lone young girl dwarfed by a huge spinning machine in a South Carolina factory; the young boys and girls rolling cigars in Florida; the children in an Indiana glass factory. Those images, along with the ones of the breaker boys, finally led to change.

Since its founding, the NCLC had worked to strengthen child labor laws in individual states. By the end of 1911, the group reported, 30 states had raised their minimum-age limits for child labor. But Progressives believed there was still much work to be done. In most states boys under 16 could still work inside mines. And the requirements on showing proof of age were still loose, meaning that many children younger than the legal limits continued to end up in factories and mines.

A growing number of NCLC committee members came to see that pursuing changes in the individual states was not the answer. The real change had to come from the federal government, with a national policy. In 1912 the NCLC got a boost when the government created the federal Children's Bureau. The bureau's basic job was to "investigate and report ... upon all matters pertaining to the welfare of children and child life among all classes of

An overseer at a South Carolina mill told Hine in 1908 a little spinner "just happened in" to work at the mill.

our people." The bureau, though, was simply supposed to gather and publish information for the government. The law creating the bureau made it clear that Congress was not trying to take away the rights of the states to pass their own labor laws.

Just as today, Americans debated how much control the federal government should have over the states. And the

U.S. Supreme Court ruled that state laws could not interfere with businesses' right to hire the workers they wanted, even if they were children. Judges across the country believed in a legal concept called liberty of contract. They thought the U.S. Constitution gave all Americans, even children, the right to sign a contract or make any other agreement with any employer. With that kind of thinking, passing tougher child labor laws would not be easy.

The Children's Bureau in 1913 became part of a new federal agency, the Department of Labor. Congress wanted the new department to investigate child labor

Five-year-old Manuel stood near what Hine called "a mountain of child-labor oyster shells" in Mississippi. Hine photographed young workers in Biloxi a month after he left the coal mines.

and companies that broke laws meant to protect children. Meanwhile, the states passed new laws limiting child labor. But, as in Pennsylvania, not all states strongly enforced the laws they passed. And if a state passed laws that companies using child workers didn't like, some companies could simply move to a state with weaker child labor laws.

Congress also pressed on with the issue, and in 1916 President Woodrow Wilson signed a national child labor bill called the Keating-Owen Act. Wilson said the law would improve "the health and vigor of the country" and promote the happiness of children. The law said products

Hine photographed young tobacco workers, ranging in age from 10 to 13, in 1917. The "leaf boy" made $1.50 a day and the girls made $1.20.

PASSING OF THE BREAKER BOYS

Pennsylvania breaker boys would eventually lose their jobs to mechanical pickers.

In 1916 Florence Taylor of the NCLC returned to the anthracite region. She found far fewer boys in the breakers. Here is part of her report on "The Passing of the Breaker Boy":

"... every foreman interviewed stated that it was the intention of the company to install mechanical pickers as rapidly as possible so as to eliminate most, if not all, of the boys. ... No feeling of bitterness toward the [child labor] law was expressed by any of the foremen, and there was apparently no effort to evade it. There was some doubt expressed as to the value the school work would be to the boys but there was no feeling that the coal companies had been harmed by it. Two foremen expressed themselves as positively in favor of the law, saying that they considered it a good thing. It was hard to get older labor, one said, but he did not blame anybody for not wanting to work in the dust of the chutes."

couldn't be shipped between states or abroad if they came from mills and factories that employed children under 14 or from mines that employed children under 16.

Not surprisingly, the new federal law upset business owners, especially owners of cloth mills, which relied on child labor. The Keating-Owen Act was challenged in court, and in 1918 the U.S. Supreme Court ruled that the law was unconstitutional. The court said that banning shipping went beyond Congress' power to regulate trade. Congress then tried a new approach. It passed a law to tax goods made by companies that used child labor. But this law too was overturned by the Supreme Court.

When he photographed young Georgia mill workers in 1909, Hine said, some boys were so small they had to climb up on the frame to mend thread and put back empty bobbins.

Despite the legal setbacks, change was coming in the Pennsylvania coal breakers. After Hine's 1911 visit, the state had passed new laws requiring students to stay in school longer and limiting the hours children could work. The laws were more strictly enforced than laws in the past and seemed to have an effect. The mine operators were now taking advantage of new technology. Machines called jigs could pick slate and other rocks out of the coal. One machine could do the work of 10 boys, and the machines quickly paid for themselves. The jigs had been around since 1904, but it took several years to make them work right. It also took the pressure of the new labor laws to

In his caption for a 1913 photo of a new coal picker machine in Pennsylvania, Hine wrote that it let through only 1 percent to 2 percent of unwanted slate, compared with 15 percent to 60 percent let through by hand-picking breaker boys.

persuade more coal mine companies to use them. Around 1914 Hine created a poster using a photo of the boys at the Ewen Breaker. Next to a photo of a jig was the caption "Child Labor abolished and the work done better." His

WHAT INDUSTRY DOES WHEN COMPELLED

Helpers in Glass Factory

THE OLD METHOD
Employer said:
"Elimination of the boys would mean the ruin of the business"

THE NEW METHOD
No Boys needed—better work done

Automatic Bottle Machine

Breaker Boys picking out slate

THE OLD METHOD
The dust makes it difficult to take a photograph. Boys breathe this air ten hours a day

THE NEW METHOD
Child Labor abolished and the work done better

Machine doing same work

Hine's photos illustrated an anti-child-labor poster that urged the use of machines, not children.

point was clear—more coal companies should use the machines to end the hard lives of the breaker boys.

Yet even with progress being made, young breaker boys still worked at some Pennsylvania mines. In 1922 the Children's Bureau released a study on child labor in anthracite country. Pennsylvania state law said children under 16 could not work in mines. Children under 14 could not work as breaker boys. But as in the past, the study found, some children got around the laws by lying about their age.

The study also showed that even with more machines running in the breakers, boys still did some of the work by hand, picking out slate the machines missed. And conditions in the breakers were not always good. Black coal dust still filled the lungs of the workers, and the slate and other rocks still cut the boys' hands. "The first few weeks after the boy begins work," the study said, "his fingers bleed almost continuously, and are called 'red tops' by the other boys."

The effort to pass new child labor laws continued. During the early 1920s, Congress approved a proposed amendment to the Constitution that would give Congress the power to regulate labor for workers under 18. But the proposed amendment needed to be approved by at least 36 states, and the effort fell short by eight states.

In 1929 the United States entered the Great Depression, its worst economic downturn ever. Three years later voters elected Franklin D. Roosevelt president. Roosevelt was

"The first few weeks after the boy begins work, his fingers bleed almost continuously, and are called 'red tops' by the other boys."

BREAKER BOY TO LABOR CHIEF

William B. Wilson served as secretary of labor from 1913 to 1921.

William B. Wilson, the first head of the U.S. Department of Labor, knew something about breaker boys and their lives. Wilson had come from Scotland to America in 1870. His father worked in Pennsylvania mines that produced bituminous coal. When he developed a disease, his son went into the mines to earn money for the family. William was just 9 when he started working, and he was a breaker boy before taking on other jobs at the mine. Unlike most of the breaker boys, however, Wilson had some schooling and continued to educate himself at home. He eventually became one of the leaders of the United Mine Workers, a union that sought better pay and working conditions for miners. Wilson also served in Congress for six years before taking his position at the Department of Labor.

During the Great Depression, Hine photographed workers at Connecticut's Shelton Looms.

willing to use the power of the federal government to help the economy and help solve social problems, such as child labor. One of Roosevelt's programs, created by the National Industrial Recovery Act, was the National Recovery Administration. This agency dealt with labor issues in general and child labor in particular. It created rules for companies to follow. Children under 16 could not work in

THE POWER OF PICTURES

The photos of Lewis Hine, who posed for a portrait in 1930, showed the dignity of working people, young and old.

Lewis Hine discussed his ideas about social photography in 1909 and showed some of his photos. Here is part of what he said in a speech:

"Whether it be a painting or a photograph, the picture is a symbol that brings one immediately into close touch with reality. ... [The] picture continues to tell a story packed into the most condensed and vital form. In fact, it is often more effective than the reality would have been, because, in the picture, the non-essential and conflicting interests have been eliminated. The picture is the language of all nationalities and all ages. ...

"The artist, [Edward] Burne-Jones, once said he should never be able to paint again if he saw much of those hopeless lives that have no remedy. What a selfish, cowardly attitude!

"How different is the stand taken by [author Victor] Hugo, that the great social peril is darkness and ignorance. 'What then,' he says, 'is required? Light! Light in floods!'

"The dictum, then, of the social worker is 'Let there be light;' and in this campaign for light we have for our advance agent the light writer—the photograph."

any manufacturing or mining jobs. No one under 18 was allowed to work in especially dangerous jobs, such as logging trees. Children from 14 to 16 years old could work in less dangerous jobs only for three hours per day and when schools were not in session.

As with the laws passed earlier by Congress, the U.S. Supreme Court ruled that the National Industrial Recovery Act was unconstitutional. Congress acted once again, placing limits on child labor in the Fair Labor Standards Act of 1938. This law said children under 16 could not work in many jobs. Farming was one of the major exceptions. As in the past, the law was challenged in the courts. This time, however, the Supreme Court said Congress did have the power to regulate labor as it had done by passing the Fair Labor Standards Act. For the first time, the United States had a lasting federal law that limited child labor.

The Supreme Court announced its decision on the Fair Labor Standards Act in February 1941. Lewis Hine had died just a few months earlier, unappreciated and in poverty. He had missed seeing his goal from the Progressive Era accomplished—ending child labor in the United States. After his days in South Pittston, Hine had worked for the NCLC for seven more years. He remained a photographer the rest of his life, usually taking pictures of people at work. Some shots became famous, such as his pictures of men building New York City's Empire State Building. But to most people, Hine is still linked to

For the first time, the United States had a lasting federal law that limited child labor.

Hine's 1931 photo of a steelworker, *Icarus atop Empire State Building*

Lewis Hine's haunting photos of Pennsylvania breaker boys moved a nation to act.

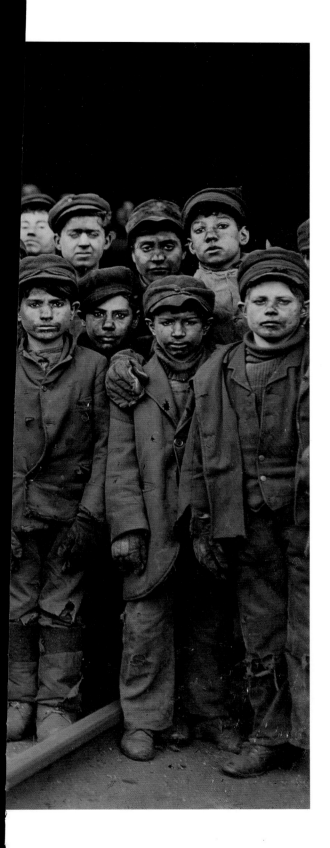

the pictures he took of child laborers. The National Child Labor Committee still exists. Each year it gives an award named for Hine to honor a person committed to helping youth.

During Hine's lifetime, his photos of the breaker boys and other children at work began appearing in books. Later weekly magazines used the photos, often to show what life had been like in the past.

Years after Hine's death, museums featured his work to show both his skill as a photographer and the history he documented. Some of the breaker boy pictures traveled around the country, giving millions of Americans the chance to see the harsh conditions children once faced at work. The image of the breaker boys, covered with coal dust, staring so hard, helped shape American history.

Timeline

Boys as young as 6 work in the breakers at the anthracite coal mines of northeastern Pennsylvania

1800s

1869

Fire at a mine in Avondale, Pennsylvania, kills more than 100 people, including boys

1905

A report by Owen Lovejoy of the National Child Labor Committee describes the conditions faced by boys working in mines and breakers

1902

The Great Strike of 1902 shows Americans that many young boys are working in coal mines and breakers

1908

Lewis Hine begins to work full time for the NCLC, photographing child laborers around the country

1911

In January Hine takes photos of breaker boys who work sorting coal in the area of South Pittston, Pennsylvania

Timeline

1912

The federal government creates the Children's Bureau to investigate child labor, among other things

1913

The Children's Bureau becomes part of the new U.S. Department of Labor

1922

A study by the Children's Bureau shows that underage boys are still working in the anthracite mines

1938

Congress passes the Fair Labor Standards Act, which includes new regulations on child labor

1916

Congress passes the Keating-Owen Act, the first national law restricting the use of child labor

The U.S. Supreme Court rules that the Keating-Owen Act is unconstitutional; Congress passes a new child labor law, but it also is overturned by the court

1918

1941

The U.S. Supreme Court rules that the Fair Labor Standards Act is constitutional; for the first time the U.S. has a lasting law that limits child labor

Glossary

amendment: formal change made to a law or legal document, such as the U.S. Constitution

anthracite: hard coal that burns slowly and gives intense heat

bituminous: relatively soft coal of a poorer quality than anthracite

captions: descriptions of pictures

census: official count of everyone living in a country; in the United States, a census is done every 10 years

collieries: sites of coal mines and the buildings used to process coal

laborer: someone who works with his or her hands

minimum: least amount acceptable

prejudice: hatred or unfair treatment toward people based on their group, race, sex, or religion

scrip: substitute for money, often a form of credit

strike: refusal of workers to do their jobs, often to protest low pay or bad working conditions

trip: train of little coal cars

unconstitutional: in conflict with the U.S. Constitution, the document that set up the government of the United States

union: group of workers who come together to try to obtain better pay and working conditions

Additional Resources

Further Reading

Bartoletti, Susan Campbell. *Growing Up in Coal Country*.
Boston: Houghton Mifflin Co., 1996.

Morris, Neil. *The Industrial Revolution*.
Chicago: Heinemann Library, 2010.

Pascal, Janet B. *Jacob Riis: Reporter and Reformer*.
New York: Oxford University Press, 2005.

Robinson, J. Dennis. *Striking Back: The Fight to End Child Labor Exploitation*. Mankato, Minn.: Compass Point Books, 2010.

Staton, Hilarie. *The Progressive Party: The Success of a Failed Party*. Minneapolis: Compass Point Books, 2007.

Worth, Richard. *Lewis Hine: Photographer of Americans at Work*. Armonk, N.Y.: Sharpe Focus, 2008.

Internet Sites

Use FactHound to find Internet sites related
to this book. All of the sites on FactHound
have been researched by our staff.

Here's all you do:
Visit *www.facthound.com*

Type in this code: 9780756544393

Source Notes

Page 4, line 6: Stephen Crane. "In the Depths of a Coal Mine." *McClure's Magazine*. August 1894. 27 April 2011. http://ehistory.osu.edu/osu/mmh/gildedage/content/CraneDepths.cfm

Page 9, line 4: Lewis W. Hine. "Social Photography; How the Camera May Help in the Social Uplift." Proceedings of the National Conference of Charities and Correction at the Thirty-sixth Annual Session held in the City of Buffalo, New York, June 9–16, 1909. 27 April 2011. http://tigger.uic.edu/depts/hist/hull-maxwell/vicinity/nws1/documents/hine-socialphotography.PDF

Page 13, line 8: "Terrible Fire in a Pennsylvania Coal Mine." *The New York Times*. p. 1. 7 Sept. 1869. 27 April 2011. http://query.nytimes.com/mem/archive-free/pdf?res=9905E4DF1431EF34BC4F53DFBF668382679FDE

Page 16, line 2: Donald L. Miller and Richard E. Sharpless. *The Kingdom of Coal: Work, Enterprise, and Ethnic Communities in the Mine Fields*. Philadelphia: University of Pennsylvania Press, 1985, p. 186.

Page 18, line 6: Walter Trattner. *Crusade for the Children: A History of the National Child Labor Committee and Child Labor Reform in America*. Chicago: Quadrangle Books, 1970, p. 26.

Page 20, line 13: "In the Depths of a Coal Mine."

Page 22, caption: "A Lonely Job." Caption for image LC-DIG-nclc-01109. National Child Labor Committee Collection, Library of Congress Prints and Photographs Division. 28 April 2011. www.loc.gov/pictures/resource/nclc.01109/

Page 23, line 5: Owen R. Lovejoy. "Child Labor in the Coal Mines." *The Annals of the American Academy of Political and Social Science*, 1906. 28 April 2011. http://books.google.com/books?id=_1I5AAAAMAAJ&pg=PA293&lpg=PA293&dq=owen+lovejoy+coal+mines&source=bl&ots=Kde_5H3jO5&sig=GBkwv5_xVEwldhI33oMoVIVnYlo&hl=en&ei=QXebTN-IIoK88gb6hKCbAQ&sa=X&oi=book_result&ct=result&resnum=7&ved=0CDQQ6AEwBg#v=onepage&q=owen%20lovejoy%20coal%20mines&f=false

Page 23, line 12: Ibid.

Page 26, line 11: Judith Mara Gutman. *Lewis W. Hine and the American Social Conscience*. New York: Walker and Company, 1967, p. 19.

Page 26, line 25: Hugh D. Hindman. *Child Labor: An American History*. Armonk, N.Y.: M.E. Sharpe, 2002, p. 91.

Page 28, line 10: "These are all breaker-boys." Caption for image LC-DIG-nclc-01117. National Child Labor Committee Collection, Library of Congress Prints and Photographs Division. 28 April 2011.www.loc.gov/pictures/resource/nclc.01117

Page 29, line 6: *Child Labor: An American History*, p. 91.

Page 29, line 10: *Crusade for the Children: A History of the National Child Labor Committee and Child Labor Reform in America*, p. 72.

Page 30, line 4: *Child Labor: An American History*, p. 95.

Page 31, line 7: Daile Kaplan, ed. *Photo Story: Selected Letters and Photographs of Lewis W. Hine*. Washington, D.C.: Smithsonian Institution Press, 1992, p. 7.

Page 32, line 7: "A view of Ewen Breaker of the Pa. Coal Co." Caption for image LC-DIG-nclc-01127. National Child Labor Committee Collection, Library of Congress Prints and Photographs Division. 28 April 2011. www.loc.gov/pictures/resource/nclc.01127/

Page 33, caption: "Noon hour in the Ewen Breaker, Pennsylvania Coal Co." Caption for image LC-DIG-nclc-01134. National Child Labor Committee Collection, Library of Congress Prints and Photographs Division. 28 April 2011. www.loc.gov/pictures/resource/nclc.01134/

Page 36, line 23: *Child Labor: An American History*, p. 99.

Page 37, caption: "At the close of the day." Caption for image LC-DIG-nclc-01104. National Child Labor Committee Collection, Library of Congress Prints and Photographs Division. 28 April 2011. www.loc.gov/pictures/resource/nclc.01104/

Page 37, line 1: *Child Labor: An American History*, p. 99.

Page 38, line 6: Ibid., p. 101.

Page 39, line 3: *Crusade for the Children: A History of the National Child Labor Committee and Child Labor Reform in America*, p. 106.

Page 39, line 15: *Child Labor: An American History*, p. 90.

Page 40, line 24: "The Children's Bureau." The U.S. Department of Commerce and Labor. Maternal and Child Health Library, Georgetown University. 28 April 2011. www.mchlibrary.info/history/chbu/20364.pdf

Page 41, caption: "A little spinner in the Mollahan Mills, Newberry, S.C." Caption for image LC-DIG-nclc-05382. National Child Labor Committee Collection, Library of Congress Prints and Photographs Division. 28 April 2011. www.loc.gov/pictures/resource/nclc.05382/

Page 42, caption: "Manuel, the young shrimp-picker." Caption for image LC-DIG-nclc-00828. National Child Labor Committee Collection, Library of Congress Prints and Photographs Division. 28 April 2011. www.loc.gov/pictures/resource/nclc.00828/

Page 43, line 10: *Crusade for the Children: A History of the National Child Labor Committee and Child Labor Reform in America*, p. 131.

Page 44, line 5: Florence Taylor. "The Passing of the Breaker Boy." Clarence Darrow Digital Collection, University of Minnesota Law Library. 28 April 2011. http://darrow.law.umn.edu/documents/Passing_of_breaker_boy_The_Child_Labor_Bulletin_1917.pdf

Page 46, caption: "Mr. A. Langerfeld and one of his machines for picking coal." Caption for image LC-DIG-nclc-05511. National Child Labor Committee Collection, Library of Congress Prints and Photographs Division. 28 April 2011. www.loc.gov/pictures/resource/nclc.05511/

Page 47, line 4: Lewis Hine. "Children Not Needed by Industry." Clarence Darrow Digital Collection, University of Minnesota Law Library. 28 April 2011. http://darrow.law.umn.edu/photo.php?pid=1172

Page 48, line 16: *Child Labor and the Welfare of Children in an Anthracite Coal-mining District*. U.S. Department of Labor, Bureau Publication No. 106. Washington, D.C: Government Printing Office, 1922, p. 16.

Page 51, line 4: "Social Photography; How the Camera May Help in the Social Uplift."

Select Bibliography

Curtis, Verna Posever, and Stanley Mallach. *Photography and Reform: Lewis Hine & the National Child Labor Committee*. Milwaukee: Milwaukee Art Museum, 1984.

Dimock, George. "Children of the Mills: Re-reading Lewis Hine's Child-Labour Photographs." *Oxford Art Journal*, Vol. 16, No. 2 (1993), pp. 37-54.

Dimock, George, et al. *Priceless Children: American Photographs 1890–1925*. Greensboro: University of North Carolina at Greensboro, 2001.

Goldberg, Vicki. *Lewis W. Hine Children at Work*. Munich: Prestel, 1999.

Gutman, Judith Mara. *Lewis W. Hine and the American Social Conscience*. New York: Walker, 1967.

Hindman, Hugh D. *Child Labor: An American History*. Armonk, N.Y.: M.E. Sharpe, 2002.

Kaplan, Daile, ed. *Photo Story: Selected Letters and Photographs of Lewis W. Hine*. Washington, D.C.: Smithsonian Institution Press, 1992.

Miller, Donald L., and Richard E. Sharpless. *The Kingdom of Coal: Work, Enterprise, and Ethnic Communities in the Mine Fields*. Philadelphia: University of Pennsylvania Press, 1985.

Novkov, Julie. "Historicizing the Figure of the Child in Legal Discourse: The Battle over the Regulation of Child Labor." *The American Journal of Legal History*, Vol. 44, No. 4 (October 2000), pp. 369-404.

Rosenblum, Walter, Naomi Rosenblum, and Alan Trachtenberg. *America & Lewis Hine, 1904–1940*. Millerton, N.Y.: Aperture, 1977.

Sampsell-Willmann, Kate. *Lewis Hine as Social Critic*. Jackson: University Press of Mississippi, 2009.

Seixas, Peter. "Lewis Hine: From 'Social' to 'Interpretive' Photographer." *American Quarterly*, Vol. 39, No. 3 (Autumn 1987), pp. 381-409.

Trachtenberg, Alan. *Reading American Photographs: Images as History, Matthew Brady to Walker Evans*. New York: Hill and Wang, 1989.

Trattner, Walter. *Crusade for the Children: A History of the National Child Labor Committee and Child Labor Reform in America*. Chicago: Quadrangle Books, 1970.

Index